D*CK & DONUTS

A CONJECTURED COLLECTION OF HOW STUDS AIN'T SH*T

by Menge Browner

I dedicate this book to every black femme lesbian who has ever rode passenger-seat around a city she loved next to a stud she was madly in love with and prayed that, this time, it actually was happily ever after. And to every black femme lesbian who is still waiting on that ride.

I dedicate this book to the woman I fell for Summer 18', Bunbae. You were my lighthouse. I could always feel the path to being a writer under my feet. I knew I was a writer but I didn't know the next step. Your light illuminated the path. Can you feel this, this book you're holding in your hands?!?! It really happened! Your encouragement inspires me the same way the sun gives flowers something to reach for.

Finally, I dedicate this book to Summer '18 and all the woman we love, have loved, and desire to love.

Table of Contents

by the dozen (intro) - pg 9

dear femme sisters . . . (1) - pg 21

ouch! y'all niggas hurtful . . . (2) - pg 39

Cinderella Effect. (3) - pg 57

they don't let go of her . . . (4) - pg 71

pain is the currency for healing. (5) - pg 83

hello, big homie . . . (6) - pg 101

her name means charming . . . (7) - pg 113

INTRO

by the dozen . . .

INTRO

by the dozen . . .

WHERE the hell did #dick&donuts come from?
So, since I started using the hashtag and saying dick and donuts people have been asking, "What the hell does that even mean?"

First, let me not take credit for coming up with the creative brilliance that is dick and donuts.

I was going through a really bad bout of depression (more on that later) and I was watching a lot of TV. A character was asked about her diet and how she was able to stay in shape and her response was, "I don't know, dick and donuts." I laughed when she said that. Hard, pure, genuine, and uncontrollable laughter. Before that, I hadn't laughed—really laughed—in a while. It was a wonderful moment and message for me. It spoke to the type of freedom I desired. No diets, no shame, no explanation. Just a tattooed, black woman speaking her truth. I dared to imagine that I could be so bold one day. I had the tattooed, black woman part down, but what in the hell was my truth?

The truth is that I was tired. Tired of being sad. Tired of hating the only body I have. Tired of straight people dominating conversations and literature on love and life. And just so very fucking tired of these fucking studs. So, I decided to adapt dick and donuts as a life motto.

About the Dick. The "dick" in dick and donuts can mean a few things. Obviously, our first thoughts go to a shafted instrument used for penetration. And then tongues, strap-ons, vibrators, tongues, fingers, whatever your creative mind can think of—and of course tongues. While all these things (used with precision) can be wonderful, the dick is wherever your sexual liberation lives. Dick, for some, may be having sex on the first date without concern as to whether she'll respect you tomorrow. For others, dick may be practicing celibacy and choosing not to let anyone into their intimate space. The "dick" in dick and donuts is defined by whoever is living the motto. Also, as a society, we have linked clothing and sexuality. So the "dick" in dick and donuts is also is also about presentation and expression. In dick and donuts, dick is your unashamed, liberated pleasure source.

About those donuts. Aren't donuts wonderful? They are the most beautiful pleasure. Technically, they are a fried food, but they behave like a wonderful baked pastry. Donuts aren't limited by how we think they should behave. You simply enjoy donuts, you don't question them. Donuts are acceptable for breakfast and after dinner; there is no time when donuts are not acceptable. They are limitless and unique. Even when they are all the same flavor, they are never uniform. Whatever it is about you that is often misunderstood, that doesn't behave or present the way the world thinks it should are your donuts. Your art, your hustle, your indulgence are your donuts. Sometimes you share but you don't have too because those are your donuts!

So, I started to think about my own dick and donuts. I questioned what I knew and what I wanted to know about love, friendship, happiness, and my place in society. I decided black lesbians needed to take up more space. Specifically, black, urban, femme=identified, stud-loving, lesbians. I started sharing my ideas online. Using the hashtag #studsaintshit, I joked about everyday dynamics between stud/femme lovers. Femmes loved it. The likes, shares, and love started to include story-sharing. My social media became a meeting ground for femmes to laugh and agree, while studs found their way to my page to argue with me or private message me that nobody is ever going to want my bitter, loud-mouthed ass, before they hit on me shortly after. What was happening though, was the creation of a space for us. We were talking about us! For the good and the bad, we were talking and we were the topic. That is what I always wanted.

Why is this so femme/stud?
The black lesbian community is small, including but not limited to your loud and proud activist/artist, out, "I just want a normal family life" folks, closeted members, bi sisters, club heads, hopeless romantics, and, of course, the fuckbois. With that context, understand that I'm writing this from a narrow perspective. Before the woke-patrol calls me out for my limited description of the community, know that I am writing this from a very femme/stud-interaction lens. I understand that many other dynamics are present in our community. For fear of leaving anyone out I will not attempt to name them. I am choosing to limit this to femme/

stud relationships because it is the dynamic I am familiar with. I believe there are countless stories that need to be told. Hell, I want to read them. But I am only an expert of my own experience. I am a femme-identified lesbian who dates, loves, and hates masculine-presenting lesbians, often referred to as studs (doms, masculine of center, MOC women). That is the story I am able to tell and, with your continued reading, the story you choose to immerse yourself in.

Every marginalized community should tell their own story. In order for stories to be authentic, informative, accurate records of history, they must be captured by members of that community. I am a stud-loving, black femme and studs are connected to my experience with love. I am a black femme. I'm telling this story how I see it. How I call it. How I live it.

If you like women that look like men, and if you complain about studs so much, why not date men or femmes?

Pause. I am attracted to women and I am attracted to masculinity. If this is a hard concept for you to grasp, it is probably because you believe that masculinity is the sole possession of men, and expressed femininity is a duty of women. Let's talk about that.

Masculinity is a set of characteristics that include but are not limited to presentation (style of dress), mannerisms, interest, assumed household duties, etc. Let me also say this definition of masculinity is defined by widely accepted social norms and is by no means science.

My personal definition of masculinity includes energy. I feel a certain type of energy from masculine people and an entirely different energy from my feminine counterparts. This energy is complex and doesn't just present itself in one way. Sometimes that energy is good masculine energy and sometimes it's that toxic shit we all know too well. Whether it be good or bad, masculine energy is its own thing. Whether it comes from a man or a woman, it is distinctive.

So to answer the question, I am emotionally and romantically attracted to women. I can only fall in love with the essence of a woman. And I am attracted to the strength of masculine presentation.

Why am I still dating them? This is a question rooted in homophobia. Straight men aren't expected to stop dating women when women hurt them. I have been asked this question by straight people and femmes who date femmes. Straight people cannot understand why I am dating a woman. They believe that straight is what is normal. So, if dating women is not this fun and carefree experience, why not just be normal? They think being gay is something you do for fun. Like drunk white girls in college listening to Katy Perry.

News flash: hurt, disappointment, anger, or frustration doesn't change someone's sexuality. I believe femme-loving-femme attraction is different from stud-loving-femme attraction. I can appreciate that their attraction is drawn to femininity. Again, this is a dynamic I would love to read about, but that ain't my story.

Why do you use nigga so much?

I don't think we need to get into a major discussion about the racial implications of the word. As a black woman, the use of the word extends beyond race and has gender implications within the black community. For example, if I say, "It's a room full of niggas, no bitches in sight," that translates to there only being men in that room. Getting into the whole "studs think they are men" shit, my theory is that men are not accustomed to seeing healthy displays of masculinity and they are confused by studs, so they do a projection reverse and accuse studs of wanting to be men. Real quick, men reading this: Fuck y'all. Don't nobody wanna be y'all weak asses.

My use of the word when I'm discussing femme/stud relations has a couple explanations. The first reason is kind of logistic; it allows for flow in a conversation. As you can guess, when having a conversation about multiple lesbians, there is a lot of "she" and "her" used. It helps if I say "sis" I'm referring to a femme sister and "these niggas" when I'm referring to studs.

The second reason is rooted in my urban heritage. It is important that we acknowledge that being urban has generational implications, traditions, language, etc. Being urban is more than a disposition, it is a culture. Language is a large part of that culture. We can understand the relationship between two people by the titles they use to address one another. Simply put, if I say mom, you can assume some things about that relationship. Similarly, urban women clearly define their relationships by the titles they use to address their partners. Girlfriend is different from fiancée; boyfriend is different from baby daddy. We may define our relationships with terms like dating, talking, kicking it, etc. But there is something lovingly possessive about referring to your lover as *"my* nigga." When you hear an urban woman say "my nigga" please understand that person is "bae" and she'll run down on you about that one. For me and my house, I'm going to say nigga long as these niggas are nigga-ing. Period.

So, (they ask me) how do you stay away from fuckbois?
One thing I love about the woke-movement is that we are talking about unhealthy relationships. We are discussing toxicity, boundaries, gas lighting, verbal abuse, and everything in between. My issue with the folks that are creating the standards and defining what healthy looks like is . . . you guessed it: *Issa buncha white academics.* They have no clue what it is to share in an experience of love as a black urban woman. How could they? (Why would they?) Their experience starts from a different place. Their definitions are influenced by their whiteness. They can't define *our* healthy because they can't understand our culture. Looking at it this way, *you* must imagine *your* definition of healthy. White academia can't do it and neither can I.

You are looking for a road map on how to avoid fuckbois? Let me kill your expectations: This ain't it, sis. This will not be a spiritual journey on how I learned to love myself and set hard boundaries. If you keep attracting fuckbois, there is something about their asses that you like. That is for you to figure out, sis. One day I had to ask myself, what did I need to feel love? What did I need in a relationship that would encourage me to dream of forever with a nigga?

I realized some of my list would not fit neatly on a "healthy relationship graph." Honestly, I like women who make me feel a little unsure of myself. Who make me pull out everything in my closet, toss it around deciding nothing is beautiful. (Not even me.) I love women that I need to fuss about my hair and makeup, for her to barely notice. Women who remind me of the men in my family, abrasive but charming, and protective as hell. Even if that protection is rooted in ownership. Women so arrogant, when we go out to eat we need a third seat for her ego. Women whose self-righteousness changes the temperature in my home when she enters. I understand that this may not be the "healthiest" formula. However, this is what I like. This ignites my passion and my interest. This wets my pussy. I have accepted my desires for the good and the bad. I know what parts of me they feed. And I also require balance. For all that ego, I need twice the hustle. For all that confidence, I must feel supported.

So, to answer my most asked question, how to stay away from fuckbois? Sis, stop dating studs. That's all you can do. They are all fuckbois or fuckbois in recovery (who still practice at least one or two fuckboi-isms). You can't avoid them. You can decide what you want, what you need, and what you are willing to accept. You cannot tell these niggas what they can and cannot do. You can decide what they won't do to you. Once you know your formula stick to it and accept nothing less.

Get yo' dick and donuts...

All this AAVE...whew, Chiiiiiiilllleeeeeee...

You will notice use of African American vernacular English throughout the book. You will also notice terms that are reserved for use in the black and or gay communities. Basically, a meal of black girl magic with a side of urban gay. I will not say I was intentional about using AAVE. One doesn't have to be intentional about their native tongue. In fact, if America wasn't so damn racist, I would be considered bilingual. Gentrification has taught me to stop calling urban shit ghetto and start appreciating undisrupted displays of black urban culture. Including our language.

I was intentional about not silencing my tongue. Most of the literature I have ever read or thought about reading about black folks is centered on oppression. Most of the LBGTQ literature I have read is created by white academics, with the intention of explaining queerness to straight people. Much of the literature (outside of poetry) I have read from black women has been almost completely void of AAVE. I want to acknowledge all black women ain't urban. So the absence of AAVE in the works of those writers is understandable and honest. However, I would guess that many of us are often subconsciously fighting stereotypes about the intelligence and abilities of black women, singing every opportunity to prove ourselves as "good" writers.

I decided, fuck all that. I am writing about black urban lesbians for black urban lesbians. If anybody else wants to read it that is fine. I will not code switch. I will not cater to the ignorance of straights or whites. The point of this work and the works of so many marginalized people is to make more space in the world for the minority groups the artist is a member of. Welcome to an unrestricted, black, urban, lesbian space. It is our time.

ONE

dear femme sisters . . .

ONE

dear femme sisters . . .

femme /fem/
noun (informal)
> A lesbian whose appearance and behavior is seen as traditionally feminine.

FEMME, the feminine presenting lesbian. We lose and gain footing depending on where we are standing. There are gender-non-conforming lesbians who accuse us of playing into heterosexual male fantasy. Who call us part of the problem and announce our privilege concerning our ability to pass for straight. Others love our energy and our representation of womanhood and femininity. Our presentation causes issues in multiple ways. We "look" (so to speak) like straight women. Which means the masculine women we attract are usually attracted to straight women. Which also means that at some point in their love journey they got played by a straight woman who spent a summer or two using them as a faux man after getting played by her baby daddy. In fact, the pushback I always get from studs when reminding the world of their ain't-shitness is, "What about femmes?" They then go on to tell me a story about getting played by a feminine, (and I cannot stress this enough) STRAIGHT woman. Now, I get it ...sexuality is fluid blah blah blah... I understand what the straight woman gets out of it. But, for the life of me, I cannot understand why studs are so obsessed with straight women since they cannot actually respect the stud as they would a man, BECAUSE THEY ARE STRAIGHT.

The relationship provides a situation where they get the love and attention we all seek but with the safety net of going back to their real world once the stud has bandaged them up—or they baby daddy gets out of jail...whichever comes first. This leaves the stud, who (sadly and pathetically) thought they were in a real relationship, in the situation. For her it was very real...but it leaves her broken. And then, here comes her broken ass, denouncing straight women and searching for a femme to drop all that hurt on. We get the damage but we do not get our due.

Femme sisters, we are a small group. This makes us limited edition: niggas love limited editions. We offer a very particular type of love, that only we can provide. We love women with our whole selves. We love women as their whole selves. Studs should love us better as we are the only people who can love them fully. We desire their femininity while honoring their masculinity. We are not using them as substitutions for anything; we see and want them for who they are. Even with all their issues. Even through their inability to love us back.

We need to reclaim our power. We have made it too easy and comfortable to play us—to play with us. If they are not willing to return the love they get from us, it is time to divest in these niggas. I know that is hard to consider but if you date studs, you are accustomed to making hard decisions by now.

The general public is heteronormative. We are surrounded by straights. Straight TV, straight books, straight Valentine's Day cards. Straight culture. But we do not call it straight culture because we have accepted straight as the norm. Black lesbians do not get enough representation. When we are featured in mainstream productions we are almost always paired with white women. Unlike our stud counterparts, we cannot recognize each other as lesbians in public settings. No matter how successful and visible we may be in our worlds, we are still the invisible lesbian. I want to acknowledge that many folks consider straight passing to be a privilege. While I agree that in impersonal interactions our presentation may provide a form of safety that masculine women aren't privy too, I would not call invisibility safety, nor is it what we seek. We are women, we are lesbians, and we do not want to be invisible. Maybe that is part of the rational with dating studs. It increases your visibility as a lesbian. Being in public with your partner unmasks a part of your identity that doesn't present itself when you are alone. The relationship offers some validation. I wonder, if this scares us into holding on in situations we should let go of? Losing the relationship, losing that stud counterpart can feel like losing yourself. You will lose some visibility. You will passively and unwillingly be closeted by your own style and presentation. I am sure there are countless reasons, but I wonder how often and to what degree this happens?

Regardless of how it happens, it happens. So, I use my platform to increase femme visibility. What happens in my "stud bashing" is not just one black femme joking and talking shit but a space being created for all black femmes. It is not just because these studs ain't shit, because at the end of the day we still fucking with them and their moves affect us. No one wants studs to get themselves together more than me/us. We laugh, agree, disagree, share, like, love the studs ain't shit discussions. More importantly we find each other. Our souls are bound in sisterhood. Even if it's over the shared hurt we've experienced through similar stupid choices in love and life, we heal together every time we laugh at studs and ourselves. I shall make more space for us wherever I go in the world. I know I drag studs a lot but, I meant every word. Fuck. Them. Niggas....

This chapter is for us... #morespace #femmesisters

So anyway sis, about these weak-ass, shrimp dick energy studs...Excuse me, what's shrimp dick energy? I'm glad you asked.

Shrimp Dick Energy

Shrimp dick energy is a phrase used to describe masculine traits that are weak and undesirable. Whenever I hear/see a stud complaining online about how femmes never take studs out to dinner, or femmes never pay for anything I nearly die of laughter. I will be the first to admit, generally speaking, femmes can be some of the most wasteful creatures on the planet. In one calendar year we spend upwards of a thousand dollars on nails...nails alone. When we go out to dinner with our homegirls we fight over the check. Once I bought a dog bowl because the font was cute...I don't have a dog. Studs with big dick energy don't have these problems. You wouldn't know it because they don't brag about regular shit, and women expressing gratitude or love byway of gifts and dinner is never major. But you shrimp dick energy conductors got all the complaints. The sad news? There are more SDE niggas than BDE niggas. So sometimes, out of availability we date y'all. (Yeah, I know, and I am disgusted.) But just because we date y'all don't mean we like y'all. Going out with a nigga with shrimp dick energy is already emotionally taxing. We are not paying for anything else. If you are in fact a stud that never gets taken out or surprised with those little "just because" gifts, sorry to break it to you, fam... you got shrimp dick energy.

Shrimp dick energy niggas tend to be angry often. They don't dominate the space with their presence so they try to overcompensate with intimidation. This anger is usually accompanied with jealousy. All the jealousy. There's the jealousy you'll recognize because of them questioning, "Who you wearing that for? Why this stud liking your Facebook pics? Whaaaa whaaaa whaa..."

Then there's that ugly, very dangerous inter-relationship ealousy that won't announce itself so readily. SDE niggas know that you could and should do better. This knowledge causes them to feel threatened by any progression or glow you exude. You get a promotion at work, they start arguments before you have go in.

You take a girls trip, they accuse you of hoe'n. You start planning to pursue your dream, they start telling you all the reasons that it is a bad idea. These niggas are not only stressful, they can become abusive and limiting. The abusive may or may not be physical.

Shrimp dick energy niggas are small, in terms of significance. They know they have not done the work to harness power in the space around them, so they need you to be small for them. To give them the illusion of having power, or to have it—but only over you. That's enough for them. They may get this power from violence or playing victim. Two sides of the same shrimp coin. If you find yourself shrinking in an attempt to fit next to them, let that shrimp go, sis.

Big Dick Energy
As with all energies, shrimp dick energy has a balancer, a counterweight if you will: The amazing phenomenon that is BIG DICK ENERGY. Big dick energy is everything shrimp dick energy wishes it could be. It fills the room. Big dick energy announces itself subtly but without question. You ever notice how some studs walk near you or stand near you and you suddenly feel free? When big dick energy is in the room your problems shrink and your capabilities magnify. Studs with this energy don't just allow you to share in their power, they teach you how to access your own. I dated a woman whose big dick energy was unmatched. She spoke so much life into me I was motivated by her silence. I knew the power in her mouth, even when her lips were still and her tongue silent. The energy was so powerful that even in her absence I knew what she would have said.

They allow this energy to speak for itself. They don't participate in boasting and peacocking. They are aware of how they dominate a space. This awareness causes them to be romantically attracted to strong, successful, talented women. They want to experience some of the unwavering strength they provide. Big dick energy is about justifiable confidence.

The energy is in every move they make, like their hugs. Niggas with big dick energy convey with a hug what others can't even communicate with sex. Their hugs say, "There is so much strength here. I'm giving you what you can handle." They do this sway rock motion when hugging, I think it's so you don't completely lose consciousness. The release is science; they let go one second before it becomes sensual. It is fucking incredible. I had an amazing conversation with artist/activist BL Bronsun concerning Big Dick Energy. I loved her perspective on the whole theory. I asked why she thought women were drawn to BDE. She responded, "It provides a space for ladies to express their femininity." That statement held so much power for me as a feminine woman. There are not enough spaces to be expressly feminine. I do not just mean be of feminine presentation. But to be feminine in expression, in spirit, to project feminine energy, without concern for safety.

But when you have a lover who has BDE that force field around them is sacred space for femininity. So, you want them around because it is in the presence of their masculine energy that your femininity is safe—protected. This energy is so powerful, but so dangerous. More than not, when it comes to relationships, studs use their power for evil. Niggas that have BDE are aware that they have it. I don't know if they truly understand what it feels like for feminine women. I also don't believe they give a fuck. What they do know is that it makes us chase them, want them, need them. So, they treat us however the hell they want to. That may be wonderful or it may be horrible but it will be whatever they want it to be. The strongest of us femmes are at its mercy. Our femininity is drawn to it, our femininity is heightened in its presence. It is less about who the stud is and more about how she allows you to be more of yourself.

How incredible it is to love a stud whose energy allows your femininity to flourish without hesitation. To exist in an energy field so big that your own growth is without limitation. If you find yourself here, know that nothing this amazing is gifted without sacrifice. It's worth it though. Worth it AF, sis.

Words of last

The last time that nigga played you
Could really be the last
If you just let it

There is no text message that is going to remind her of your humanity
No sub-post that will demand she offer you yo' due respect
There will be no sudden epiphany in her
Concerning you

Sis, I am a writer
And not much more
So I believe in the impact of words
I know their power
Words sustain me
So I know
What you want yours to do
To her
For you
In this situation

I'll tell you
When it comes to conflict
Kingdoms at war
Are more gentle with their words
Than lovers who harbor resentment
Than niggas, who ain't shit

And sis, that nigga ain't shit

See I want to poem this thing you're going through right now
Wanna roses are red violets are blue
Have a good cry and learn to love you
Self-care you to death
Riddle you with metaphors
Wrap you in parables
Rock you to a haiku heaven
Where consistency and honesty are built in

But that ain't shit nigga you crying about
Ain't worth all that energy
Not on my part or yours

The only one here that gets your attention tonight is you
Instead why isn't she calling
Ask yourself why you're even waiting
Is she actually that incredible
Or are you just that lonely
Do you need her voice to pollute the air
Until there is no room for your own thoughts
Has her pollution been around so long
You find a landfill more comfortable than your own bed
Wait...I said I wasn't going to poem this
But sis…
Have you romanticized this nigga, maybe just a little?
Maybe….

The last time you got played
Could really be the last time
If you just let it

Unlike most journeys

Leaving a fuckboi doesn't start with the first step
It starts with the first not
Not calling back
Not responding
Not checking their social media
Not wishing/praying/chanting
This nigga back to you

Master the not
Worry about the rest later
Your power starts with the not
This is the only moment you can control

She's left you like this 47 times
That means you can be the woman who only lets a nigga play her 47 times…

And that sounds funny, perhaps even weak the first time you say it
But doesn't it sound stronger than 48 times
And won't at some point we get it down to a single digit
Sis I ain't judging you
I'll tell you a secret

I'm terrified of winter driving
I tend to attract niggas with trucks
And excellent spin out skills
When there is ice on the ground a nigga can play me twice
3 times with good credit
4 times with good head
5 is she eat it from the back… but 5 times max
That's it

There is no need for perfection
Just some boundaries
And some not…
Not chasing these ain't shit niggas
Doesn't tell them what they not gon' do
But it will let them know who they not gon' do it to
We not tripping
At least not 48 times

Femme sisters: we have aided in some of the ain't-shitness of studs. We must acknowledge this, then take a stand. I learned a long time ago that the only woman you can actually control is yourself. So instead of telling niggas what they not gon' do, lets agree on what we not gon' do, accept, or respond to. Sisters I give to you the "we not" agreements. Speak them aloud when you need to.

We not
Questioning our self-worth because of another person's behavior.
Their behavior is a reflection of who they are not who you are. If they cheat it is because they are a cheater not because you are unworthy of honesty and commitment. Your worth does not change because of another's inability to see it.

Dating studs that call women "females"
That is that on that...

Getting rid of stud friends for our partners insecurities.
Now sis, do not go stretching the word friend...I am talking actual platonic friends. Not waiting for they chance, hating, low-key flirting niggas that you call bro.
Always be respectful while being mindful that catering to insecurities will have you in a never-ending cycle of losing everything around you. You are allowed to be friends with whoever brings your life joy.

Chasing these niggas.

I've learned that if she wants you she will come get you, or minimally meet you. But when you chase a nigga you get tunnel vision; then you cannot see all the better niggas. Be still and know that you are a goddess.

Waiting on them to make the first move.
Go for what you want. Or you'll end up with a nigga that chose you, not the nigga you want. The fact is we are invisible, studs don't know if we're lesbians, if we're single, if we're interested. It is okay to slide in a nigga DM; just do so with feminine grace. Try not to embarrass the team coming on too strong with the extra thirsty comments. If y'all are online friends, find a mutual interest and start a conversation. You're welcome.

Dating broke studs.
I know how this sounds. This ain't about gold-digging. But the reality is if she is broke, it is going to cost you. If she is broke, she needs to be hustling getting her affairs in order and put dating on the back burner. I once had a woman tell me, "When we first met I wanted to date you but I ain't have my shit together enough to try you." This remains one of my favorite compliments. It says she respected me enough not to ask me to join in holey mattress-on-the-floor with her. Furthermore, poverty is stressful; it is going to stress the relationship and boffa y'all. Say no to broke.

Saving egos in the bedroom
If she can't fuck, she can't fuck. Stop suffering through sorry strap. Quit faking fingering orgasms. Leave wack head on "read". We

really be gassing these niggas. And for what? It is our fault. We faked orgasms, throwing pillows and shit. Then the relationship ends and the nigga out here telling her new bitch how she had you moving furniture. Sis, it can't get better unless you address it. This is hard, I know. ALLLL studs think they the shit in the bedroom, it's truly exhausting. They may reject the conversation at first with the "I ain't never had no complaints before" argument. Remind her that this is not before, this is right now. Then be honest, with your words and reactions. She can't argue that body language.

Waiting on niggas
Not to get they shit together. Not to call us back. Not to pick us up. Issa no. Period. The beast in me will tell you, fuck these niggas. There's always a better nigga—or, at the very least, another nigga. The lady in me will tell you, your time is so valuable. When we wait on them, we wait intently. This must stop. If you must wait, do so passively. Work on the project you've been thinking about; go to brunch with your homegirls; visit grandma; go shopping. Do something; be out in the world. Let these niggas know your time and attention are not infinite.

Competing with each other
First off, issa nuff' niggas for everybody. Be mindful of falling into the "last nigga on earth" syndrome. Competing with other femmes pedestals these niggas. They ain't the prize and this ain't the damn Olympics. Love, forgive, and treat your femme sister half as good as you treat niggas that make you cry and repost

emotional memes.

Defending our desires
Listen for the fear behind their statements. If a stud tells you "you want too much," hear the "I'm unable to live up to your expectations." There is no such thing as wanting too much. You want what you want; you are allowed to want what the fuck you want. Anyone you date can decide not to provide those wants and move on. But never shrink your desires to fit into her hands, if she cannot hold all of you…

New Nigga me, please…

TWO

ouch! y'all niggas hurtful . . .

TWO

ouch! y'all niggas hurtful . . .

THE FUCKBOI Dating Experience

But why do we keep dating fuckbois you ask? It's simple really. Fuckbois date. Well.

They call with plans and instructions. They ask women out. They take women on goddamn dates. The average masculine stud has no clue how to date. There, I said it. I could go on and on with some elaborate explanation why (most) studs are absolutely horrible at dating but I'll be brief. Studs are women, who were once little girls. This means they were socialized the same way as femmes: raised to be pursued and courted. This socialization creates a stud who can't lead when dating because she was trained to follow. I say most studs because, thank heaven it ain't all. There are the few that have been able to disregard the socialization and training for womanhood they received in their youth. Some (very few) have learned to navigate dating. Sadly, most of the champion "daters" are fuckbois. To be clear, anything you do a lot, you tend to do well. Fuckbois date a lot of women. This keeps them out in the world socializing often. They know all the new restaurants and get preferential treatment at all the old spots. They want to control situations so they always want to drive, don't mind planning, and are ready to pay. Fuckbois try new food, have no issues meeting (and charming) your homegirls, and have the best conversation...these niggas are funny and smart.

They know how to customize their interactions for the individual women in their lives. They go into dating experiences knowing that it is only a temporary experience. So, they treat it as such. For short term daters, the experience is more like a vacation than an investment. They can set high standards because they only need to be able to keep up with themselves for a few months. Meaning if they do something really nice like, pay your car note, or take you on a trip, they aren't concerned about this setting an expectation. They won't be around to deal with your disappointment anyway.

This is not to say every champion "dater" is a fuckboi. I am saying their experience gives them a leg up. They can also operate in that space differently because they don't have the same pressure on them as people who are dating to find a long-term partner.

I am not fully against dating fuckbois, for all the aforementioned reasons. You are just going to want to date them in a way that serves you. Allowing a fuckboi to compliment and charm you can be good for the soul. They are wonderful with assisting in transitioning out of a relationship back into the jungle of being single. However, you need to go into it aware that you are accepting an unspoken agreement of it being a short-term experience. With that firmly in your mind, heart, and spirit, enjoy every moment—but let those moments pass without seeking to contain them. You cannot hold on to a moment or a fuckboi; they are both fleeting and beyond the restriction of your desire. Again, date them for you, not for them. This is definitely easier said than done. All the things that allow fuckbois to get away with being fuckbois are things that will make you fall, fall, fall.

Now, in case a self-proclaimed "good guy," stud head-ass is reading this about to sing the "women don't like good guys" song: We like good guys. We don't like boring-ass, can't plan a night, unable to take charge, unsure, nervous, ain't never been nowhere, don't smell like Chanel, needy, looking bois. All fuckbois are not bad people. And most definitely, all "good guys" are not good partners. In fact, the very idea that women owe you some type of attention because of who you ARE NOT instead of who you are, actually exposes your petty heart and cancels out your "good."

But to the point: We enjoy dates. Fuckbois date well. And here we are...

More about Saturday
(They don't Netflix and chill you to death.)

What qualifies as a date? That's a question each femme has to ask herself. Because dates should be specific to the woman being courted, what one sees as a date may not be a date to another femme. There is a difference though between a date and spending time together. This can be confusing, as one of the functions of a date is to spend time together; however, a date requires a sacrifice. Money, time, thought. All these things are sacrificial. Also, if you are dating to find a partner, you need to know this motherfucker can plan a night out. Trust me, you do not want to plan a life with someone who can't plan a night out. A lot of these studs are still walking around with open wounds from the straight girl that played them and snatched all their coins. So, by the time you find their asses, they're all weird and selfish with their time and money. These wounded studs want you to earn a date. Fuck these niggas. Do not perform for them; do not allow them to waste your time. These are lil' niggas. Find a Big Homie to date.

When Queen Charming and I first started dating she would literally make it a point to see me every day. Every day we went on a date. This is no exaggeration: every day we went on a date. Sometimes they were very long dates where we spent the entire day together. We would go to multiple locations, eat breakfast and lunch or lunch and dinner together, hours on end. Other days when our time was limited, we would go get frozen coffee and DONUTS (!) from the nearest cafe. After a few weeks of this, one day she texted me and asked if I was home so she could "pull up and see me."

I responded, "Okay, where we going?"

"Nowhere. I was just gon' pull up for a minute."

"And do what? What does pull up mean?" I wondered.

"Oooohhhhhh, you a *lady* lady. I gotta take you somewhere every time I pull up on you?" It wasn't a real question at this point.

"Yeah, but Starbucks is fine."

This is a necessary type of communication. She threw a desire out there, I responded with a boundary. She acknowledged, accepted, and (this is important) responded to my terms. I acknowledge that this was a critical moment. She could have laughed and responded, "Nah." She could have decided I was too high maintenance and stopped dating me. But having these conversations early help structure the relationship from the very beginning so that it doesn't become an issue if the relationship progresses. It was too early in our dating for a "pull up." What you do in those first months set the tone for the relationship. While there is absolutely nothing wrong with 'Netflix and chill,' it is not a date. It is something you do when you are too tired to plan a date.

Queen Charming and I have spent many a night scrolling Netflix and doing nothing more. These nights happen usually after we are both exhausted from life but desire to be close to one another. Our Netflix and chill time is important for our relationship at this point. It allows us to be close without the energy of outsiders. It allows for much needed rest but still honors the relationship as a priority. Netflix and chill happens out of necessity. It does not, however, qualify as a date and it does not take the place of a date. Queen Charming no longer has to take me out to see my face but dating…going out on dates was our beginning—our source of knowing, learning, loving each other. Whenever something is in need of nourishment you must go back to the source. Relationships have a life all their own. Anything with life needs nourishment for growth. If your source is a place of minimal effort, that is all you will ever be able to pull from it. If the source of your dating is rooted in sacrifice, time, investment, consideration, planning, and attentiveness, when those things lack, you can re-up at the source. Big Homies never neglect the source.

For Urban Women Who Love Urban Women

The little things are never little things. Something as simple as "you want something from the store" is layered with history and culture. Big Homies know that the little things matter. Here's a little story about a little love language...

Gas Station Snacks...on dating urban femmes
A bottled water. The soda I said I need to stop drinking. My favorite chips (she knows which ones). And that candy bar we both love. Similar to the need for movie concessions, Big Homies need you comfortably seated while you ride around without destination. You haven't really seen your city until you've enjoyed it passenger side to a driver who knows how to regain control in a spin-out while rolling a blunt and changing songs on their phone. All experiences are made more fulfilling with a meal: this adventure calls for gas station snacks.

Every bite of food a black person consumes is loaded with politics, history, and source. While there has been a beautiful rise in black people returning to plant-based diets, becoming pescatarian, vegetarian and vegan, some foods are ingrained in our cultural experience. We have our staples. I ain't just talking peach cobbler. Our staples are also $1 Coneys (only on Wednesday), black girls and bubble gum/sunflower seeds, red beans and rice...on top of extra rice (gotta stretch it all week), and the infamous gas station snacks.

Whenever we discuss soul food, we picture the Thanksgiving layout. Collard greens, baked macaroni and cheese, fried chicken, and all the liquid diabetes you can drink. Now, many of us refer to soul food as slave food. This has always intrigued me. We tend to say slave food with disgust. But I know there is so much life in that food. Those plates are/were an intergral part of our survival. Slave food was supposed to be just enough to keep us alive long enough to work. But we did what we always do. We got creative and made beauty out of nothingness. Our ancestors that survived slavery used food to preserve African culture, to nourish African people, and to reclaim the handing down of traditions.

While soul food has been on the menu since "Plymouth Rock landed on us," our kitchens and appetites went through another cultural shift in the 80s. The crack epidemic changed our communities but also our kitchens. Crack did something no other force of government or nature could do. Crack took mothers out the house. To an addict, drugs are more satisfying than food. Black American children, who lost their mothers to drugs, began to starve third-world style in hoods near you. Many babies born during the crack epidemic were born with symptoms of crack addiction. Sugar was used as a synthetic drug to quiet fussy, irritated, addicted babies. Boxes of government-issued, processed food, loaded with sugar became our dinner. Sugar in the water (Kool-Aid), sugar in the food, sugar in the condiments. The condiments we used excessively to make the cardboard patties taste more like...food. Dip it in ranch, cover it in ketchup, hit it with hot sauce. When culture shifts it changes what's on our plates and what we readily identify as food and food sources.

Our homes, these urban neighborhoods we are born in, like us, suffer from neglect. Abandonment and lack of common amenities are the proof. Our survival is challenged in every way imaginable. Hoods are known for being food deserts. Food desert (n) - an urban area in which it is difficult to buy affordable or good-quality fresh food. ["food desert." Lexico.com. 2019. https://www.lexico.com (16 July 2019)] Our grocery stores don't carry fresh food; the dusty ass food they do carry is marked up for people with less money. Almost everything comes in a box, bottle, can or sealed bag. We see labels, not food. So, our subconscious reads labels as an answer to hunger. While this happens in rural areas they respond with general stores. In suburban areas their chain pharmacies boast grocery sections that shame our actual grocery stores. In our neighborHOODS, our answer to quick convenient food is the local gas station. Gas stations give us the snacks, comfort, convenience, and familiarity we need and desire.

These food struggles keep us consistently in survival mode. Survival mode causes us to think of food, shelter, money, etc. all the time, taking up brain space and making emotional needs secondary. Making love secondary. We are so guarded, operating almost tactical style. We are in a concrete jungle that only the strong will survive. And love can be perceived as weakness, meaning love is weakness. So, open displays of love aren't taught or encouraged in traditional ways. Also, sometimes urban women are too deep in survival mode to fully appreciate traditional methods of expressing love. This is not to imply urban woman don't enjoy roses. But urban women must be loved in practical, beautiful ways. Removing some of her need is the only way to allow her to fully engage in her desires. Loving us isn't hard, it requires strategy. We want displays of love that we can read. Nothing reads more poetic than, "I'm on my way. You need something from the gas station?"

Count

My door is literally 17 steps away from my bed
On nights I crave you inside of me more than my own organs
And you come over unexpectedly
I skip
My door is 12 steps away from my bed

Nights you leave me,
With little time between my orgasm and your departure
I drag
My door is 23 steps away from my bed

You are always coming and going
Your presence never forever
But will you always come…back?

Are you training me to live in desire and absence
Or anticipation and fulfillment
Is this the balance you offer

Will your pursuit of me be as constant as your pursuit of wealth
Do I offer any value to your legacy
This is what I don't say when you visit
The time is so short
Filled with much passion
I am afraid to ask
Anything that may force an honest moment I am ill prepared for

The joy of loving a woman who chases is
Having to challenge your own endurance
The fear of loving a woman who re-ups

Is knowing everything is on a cycle
And that the beginning only makes way for the ending

Is this our beginning or ending?
Isn't it both?

I am 17,12, 23 steps away from you most nights
You are a text, a call, a pull up away from me most days
I am a woman who has counted the steps
In an effort to slow down her beating heart
In anticipation of your face
You are a woman who is so stoic
That I'll never know if you count at all

A woman who has stood 1 step away
And made me wonder if she were here at all
My bed is literally 17 steps away from my door
Whether or not you are on the other side
But anything that is not you
Doesn't invoke counting
Doesn't require a step count

Your presence demands mindfulness
Ask my feet to report to my soul
How many more steps?
17, 12, 23

I'll keep count
In hopes that I can keep you

And all that you are

"I don't care about niggas liking my girl. Shit, I like her too."
- Queen Charming in discussion about niggas my inbox…

Spoiled

I am
Potato salad left on a picnic table
For 2 days
During a heat wave
Next to uncooked tilapia
Soaking in chunky cows milk
Spoiled

I can't see past her
Lord I don't want whatever is back there
She gotta be the one

Matter-fact I'ma make her the one
Only one I call
Only one I fuck
Only one imagine forever with

Nothing makes you a
Underwear folding
T-shirt drawer organizing
Baby, can I make you a plate
Please let me take care of the bill this time
Head-ass bitch

Quicker than a Big Homie
Or one who doesn't need her hand held
Knows how to control the energy in the room
A truck in a Detroit winter

And my MOTHA-FUCKING MOUTH

My linen closet is exceptionally neat
Because I've been folding niggas
So long
It's refreshing to love a woman without crease marks
Who doesn't bend, never folds

Her strength spoils me
So well, so well it's scary
If she ever leaves this space
I'm afraid it will be forever vacant

Standards adjusted in recognition of her actions
Standards so high
Exactly her height

Can't take no shorts now
The sun feels different
After being loved right
Can't go back to only feeling the sun in the summer

I need this heatwave
It's already spoiled me

I know what I want

I want her to be tall
Beautiful and confident
When I look up at her
I want her eyes to pull me in
And intimidate me...just slightly
When I look up at her
I need us both to silently acknowledge
That she has the power to make me fall apart
But rest assured that she wouldn't
I want her power to be undeniable

Let it take air out of the room until
She reminds me to breathe
I want her to speak so calmly
I'm reminded of resting volcanoes
Like those brief moments when the ocean stands still
But you're respectfully aware of its undercurrent

Look at me beautiful
Tell me with your eyes
How you've never seen a more captivating sight
Say "I love you" without moving your lips

I want her to be experienced in life and love
Smart enough to hold on to the lessons of the past
But let go of the women

I want her to want me

The same way we want water on hot days
Like a need that reads in the tone
Of a desire

Let her want for me
Be as my want for her
May our passion for each other
Ignite itself
Over and over
Then
Again
Heavy

THREE

Cinderella Effect.

THREE

Cinderella Effect.

THE FUNNY thing about this night is tonight was the night I was going to establish boundaries. I told her she had to leave at midnight. Of course, I didn't want her to go. But she couldn't spend the night and her 2:00 am visits confused my internal clock. I told her she had to leave at midnight, so *I'd* be the one deciding for a change, tired of the anxiety from all the what-ifs and maybes. I set an alarm; I was god damn serious. The alarm rang while we were mid-kiss. I stood up, adjusted my dress. It was form-hugging but without embellishment. One of those dresses that was an outside dress but I got some paint on it that I couldn't get out. Still a good dress for my shape so I kept it. Wore it when I wanted to look like I wasn't trying, when I was. I walked her to my bedroom door. She followed slowly, but nonetheless she followed. We kissed at the door, I clung to her—

tried to kiss her in a way that made her want to hurry back and regret having to leave at all. For good measure I lifted my leg high above her hip, rested it around her waist. Her hand found my pussy. This is the moment I discovered her fingers arch in the exact angle my g-spot sits. She didn't have to find it or go to it; there was a magnetic draw. For the life of me, I can't tell you how we ended up back on the bed. I don't remember her undressing me or herself. I do remember the candle flicker making her shadow larger than life on my wall. I watched her shadow fuck mine, until my eyes shut.

She laid with me. Held me in my post-orgasmic haze. My scent on her tongue, my lust still under her fingernails. I made the mistake of relaxing into her arms, head on her chest. I made the mistake of relaxing in my own damn bed. I drifted as she remembered... all at once. This was not her bed. I was not the woman in her bed. Just a woman she was in bed with. She had her own bed, and in it a woman who wished her there instead of here, with me. She sprung up. Our midnight was 4am, her pumpkin coach a truck, her glass slipper whichever random Harraches she wore that night. She left no glass slipper. She left a footprint on my self-worth. I watched her casual, slew-footed fuckboi gait step lightly down my steps and away from me. I watched her lights come on. Watched her drive off. Watched her... not look back. Not. Once. She sped toward the woman. I guess that's what you call her when you're 'the other.' She could look either way, backward or forward and there'd be a woman waiting for her.

How exhausting it must be to always be both, heading toward and away from a woman.

Nightmare

I'm never going to tell you about the night a nightmare woke me up
Never tell you how much I needed you, needed to hear your voice
Hear you say "it was just a dream, go back to bed, silly"

(But) I couldn't call you
It was 1am
Your phone ringing at that time would've awakened her and her suspicions

So I sat with my fear
Trying not to think about the nightmare
I thought about you
And the why I couldn't call you

And that…a whole other nightmare
The nightmare of being your other
Doesn't end when I wake
Doesn't sleep when I sleep
Doesn't take a night off

Never becomes now

She won't leave me how she found me
For the good or the bad
I'll have to reintroduce myself to myself after her
I've done all the things I said I never would
She is a slayer of nevers
Never cry all night
Never abandon my homegirls
My beliefs
Never be on call for a nigga
Who can only call when her girl at work
I've become queen of those nevers
Now…always

I want to stop but I don't
I need to stop but I won't
I almost didn't answer for her last time she called
But I did
So that almost matters not
And that pause, when I briefly considered not answering
Lost its dignity
That pause if held a little longer
Would have transformed into some fucking self-respect
But that pause held its own so briefly
Bent to her will so willingly and spineless
I call it mini me
Pause behaved just like me
Punk-ass pause
Just want somebody to love it pause

Secret pause

Bet' not tell nobody but God, it'll kill yo mama mister pause
If she ever asked
I'd lie about that pause
Throw it under the bus so fast
Tell her I've never hesitated at the ring of her call

The vibration of her nothingness fills the hungry chambers of my heart
Like nothing else
Even if this situationship is just a display of low self-esteem and nothingness
It is something
It is all I have for now
It is the never that won't let me envision my always
And I hope I never this much again

Chore of Not

Not calling is a chore
She exhausts me
In her presence
And again
In her absence

Only with fuckbois
Do you use more energy not doing something
Than actually doing something

When you decide not to call
You give up your day with the not
I am not
Gone call this nigga
Respond to that generic ass text
I won't
Check her Facebook all day
Regret not putting her in a jar when I had the chance

I will
Change my screensaver
Binge watch…everything
Dye my hair
Buy a dress
Flirt with a medium ugly stud online
Pray Fast Chant
Play lemonade on repeat
Regret not putting her in a jar when I had the chance

Waiting on daddy

I learned to wait for someone who wasn't showing up from my father. One Friday
afternoon (there were many) but this one specific Friday won't leave my mind. I remember what the sun smelled like that day. Anyway, I had on this yellow and white hand-me-down skirt set. Looking back, it was hideous, but at the time I treasured it. I had set it out on my dresser days earlier, kept it wrinkle free. See, my dad had a rule about being presentable when he came to pick us up, and so I stayed presentable.
Yellow and white barrettes
Yellow and white socks
Yellow and white skirt set
Sitting still, clutching a purple book bag.
Ignoring my play cousins calls to come and play. A good game of dodgeball would surely ruin the presentation.

I sat still.
I ignored them.
I sat still.
I fell asleep.

Woke up in my own bed. My mother must've moved me while I slept...
And now, I clutch a leather clutch. I wait inside the house, my mother too far, and far too old to carry me inside these days.
If I fall asleep waiting, Lord, please let me lay my head in a way that doesn't give me a crook in the morning.
If I fall asleep waiting, let these curls hold another day...
If I fall asleep waiting let me remember not to lay my made-up face on this new dress...

That I bought for a night out (that I stayed in)…
That I practiced my "this old thing" wave in response to your anticipated compliment.

That I prepped for days ago
Been shopping
Been curling
Been smiling
Been dreaming
Started when I was 6.
So, when you cancel, long after your scheduled arrival, it's really ok,
I'm fine with it, in fact it's my normal, my familiar.

At least I can laugh (to myself) these days. Finally understanding why women commonly refer to their partners as "daddy."
I learned to wait for someone who wasn't coming from my father.
I know if I fall asleep waiting, I'll get up again. (And again.)
But Lord when I do die
let my hair be a mess, my dress be old, let me be in need of a shower.
Let it be painfully clear that at the very least I didn't die …waiting on daddy.

Edge

I'll pick up for you when you call
When I am dangerously close to the edge
I'll pray you don't push me, please pull me back
No
Go ahead and push me, don't pull me back

I practice pretending I wasn't waiting on your call
As I wait on your call
Sometimes I do things
But only to have a story for you when you call

I answer with a controlled glee and liveliness
That confuses even myself

You send your WYD text via arrow
You're precise and deliberate
So I respond with surgical care

See I need to be busy enough that I'm interesting
But not so busy that I'm unavailable …
Not just available but easily accessible and limitlessly accommodating

You have any idea how much work it is to be a woman who requires…no work

You have any idea how illogical I must be
To let you disrupt every part of my existence in an effort to be your fucking peace

Oops did I say "fucking"
I know how much you hate it when I curse
When I behave utterly human
When I remind you that I am just a woman

Just a woman
Not a concept
Just a woman
Not even your woman

Who you complain about
Who you never said you were leaving
Who you leave to come…to me
Whose tongue you claim is always eager for war
Who you always return to
Who you make no demands of peace

I find myself jealous of a woman (I know for a fact you're cheating on)

She says "fucking"
"Where the fuck you been"
"Who you fucking"

When you respond to her
For all my effort
Do you at least tell her you left because you needed some "peace"

Or am I then
Your working late
Your gym
Your visiting yo mama

I am everything except her
She is everything except peace
But damn if you don't return (to her)
For war and for more every night

I am not your peace
At most I am an army nurse
I return you bandaged
But…to the battlefield you go

I am not your peace
For if I were
I'd tell you this…this shit is unattainable

I cannot even offer you peace
After all you see how loosely I gamble my own

FOUR

they don't let go . . . of her.

FOUR

they don't let go . . . of her.

The Mail Doesn't Run on Sunday

Your ex's mail still comes to your house
I pretend not to notice it
At least you don't leave it in plain sight on the table anymore
I pretend not to notice it come in
Not see it stuffed in the side slot of your black bag
Not see you leave with it
Then return without it

Never allowing myself to consider what happens between
Stuffing it in the side of your bag
And returning without it

Sometimes when the side slot is empty I stare at your bag
I wonder if it waits with anticipation (or if you do)
If it prays the mailman brings it an excuse bearing her name (or if

you do)

I don't ask the bag any questions
It sees more than I can bear
I don't touch the bag I clean around it
I don't believe I could lift the weight of its secrets

I hate the bag for its participation in this
Hate the mailman because I feel like he knows
Hate your ex because…how hard is it to change your fucking address
Hate everyone except you

I know you mean well
Mean not to hurt me (even when you do)
I accept the ritual of stuffing the mail in the bag
As your attempt at damage control

And that is more than any other lover has offered me
So I accept it by returning a smile upon your return
By not questioning the bag or you or….anything

Your ex's mail still comes to your house
And so do I
One day one of us
Will have to stop

FRIENDS with exes

This right here is a fuckboi calling card. Now, back—way back before my gay day, the queer community was small and operating in secret. During those days, I don't think we could afford to dispose of one another simply because a relationship ended. After all, the circles were so small and community building so necessary. I understand that, during that time, the practice of holding on was essential to our survival as a community. With that said, it is currently the Year of our Lord, 2019. We are loud and proud. And out and accounted for. Our marriages are legally recognized. We can find one another online, at clubs, at community centers, etc. I would say, at this stage of the game, this level of holding on is no longer a need for our survival as a community.

Leave it to the fuckbois, however, to selfishly use a dated survival method for their own benefit. You see, weak niggas will just lie and cheat to keep multiple women. Fuckbois, on the other hand, use their unapologetic entitlement to collect women—dead-ass in your face. Many fuckbois will tell you quite honestly that they only date one woman at a time. They like to explain how they are "too grown to be sneaking around, lying and shit." What they have managed to do though is find a way to beat the system with the infamous "I'm friends with my ex." This statement allows them to transition every woman they have ever dated and/or fucked into another one of their "good ol' friends." This then opens the door for them to have an unlimited number of women who they are emotionally entangled with in their lives.

This also aids in their ability to move on from their relationships with femmes quite easily. They never have to actually leave a woman, they only need to reposition her and make room for a new one. The steps are: befriend, date, promote-to-girlfriend, love, leave, demote-to-friend. This creates an ever-growing collection exes. This then leads to the question: Why do we allow this?

Femmes want safety, longevity, forever...we want the fairy tale. We do the dating, the loving, the waiting, in an attempt to become girlfriends or, if we dare to dream, wives. Meanwhile, studs continually change the rules of engagement. They are experts at keeping the goal post within sight but always out of reach, not to mention the brainwashing. We are hit with "Bond is better than a title" or "What's understood doesn't need to be explained" and all the other bullshit. If they can get you to agree to this shit, you then become an accomplice to your own pain. It allows them all access to you and your body—all that you are and all that you bring—without any commitment from them. You become a fun-girl. Or a woman they can call at leisure when it suits them, giving only what they choose with no concern for your needs. When a fun-girl attempts to behave like...a human, announcing any displeasure or lack of acknowledgement, note how quickly she is reminded, "You ain't even my girl." Some of us have lived entire relationships as a fun-girl. Never graduating to girlfriend; never even offered the opportunity to become an ex-girlfriend who becomes a friend.

Maybe friendship is the only version of forever studs can commit to. They are not robots and they crave human companionship like the rest of us. But they cannot be trusted with the responsibility of cultivating forever. Friendship only requires history and existence. Maybe femmes accept these "friendships" because all we ever dreamt was forever, without the specifics to make it what we truly desire. We accept friendship because after accepting so much of their bullshit we don't want to walk away with nothing. So we walk away with…a friend?

This is not Growth

How painful it must be to dig holes in your ears
Gripping shovels
Making them graveyards
For so many ex-lovers
Your left ear
Filled with soft, unpacked dirt
Where you buried the lies she told you during your relationship

Your right ear
You lend to her confessions
You hand pack regret
In your voice as you call her your... friend

How many times can you let yourself embalm the same woman
How many places will you bury her stiff words
And how long
How long do you expect me to keep trying to outlive her ghost
How many seeds must I plant amongst the dead that keeps dancing

Tales

You're going to make me one of those women in these stories you tell so well
Aren't you
I realized this
Searching for places in your scalp to massage
Carefully parting your locs

You tell me another story
(There is always a fucking story)
About yet another woman
(There is always ANOTHER fucking woman)

Sometimes the woman is the backbone
Sometimes she's merely a mention
But she's always there
Even though she changes often

This story you're telling right now
This woman
(I believe she's one from the east coast)
I don't know
Haven't been following
There are so many
I can't keep them straight anymore

There's no way for me to tell you this

So I say nothing

I think of my story

I'll never hear it
My story is for the next woman
(There will always be a next woman)
Because who are you without these stories
And who are women but mentions in your tales

I have no reason to believe I am any better
Or worse than
East coast woman West coast woman Midwest woman Hometown woman
Hometown woman's friend

I am a tale unfolding
Nothing more
Another Tale

I cannot ignore how small I am to you anymore
Even when we make lo—when we fuck
What I should enjoy, I question
Where did you learn that?
Was she before me or during my time
Do you fuck us all this way
I'm too weak for your answers

I don't ask
I love you and
I'm trying to twist my tale into something interesting
It's the least I can do
For the next woman who parts your locs
And hears what she doesn't want to know
Doesn't need to know
As she becomes a tale herself

A tale unraveling in the ears of your next women
And won't you unravel a woman
Make her a character
Just 1 part of the 5 it takes to make up a story
Arguably the most interchangeable part
Often the least important

Her back, my back, our backs
Just something to rest your plot on
You plot on women like me don't you
Poets and spiritual women
Who stay to hear the ending
Who stay trying to be your ending
Your happily ever after
But summed up in a run-on sentence

You speak with poor diction and
Lazy cadence
And I listen knowing I will end up a foot note in your "How to Play These Bitches for Dummies" workbook

So I stay and I listen
With disinterest
Passively anticipating
The End
I know I know

I know I know
You and your friend…are different
Yes she's your ex but
What you guys have now is independent of that

I know I know
There is just so…much…history
And besides
Y'all ain't like these other messy people out here
Y'all are respectful
Ain't no funny business

I know I know
You can speak for both your feelings AND HERS
Trust me I know
Oh…this is the part where you tell me
We basically family at this point
I mean family whose pussy has taken residence on your lips
But…I get it
Don't worry
Don't explain
Y'all iz different

I know
For this is the 95,658,408 time
I've heard this story
So save your energy
I know and you know and yo' ex…oh she know

FIVE

pain is the currency for healing.

FIVE

pain is the currency for healing.

Deal and Heal

She cheated. When I found out I got angry. I yelled. I screamed. I threatened. Then I got scared. What did this mean—for me and about me? Am I worthless? Am I not worth basic human kindness? Then, I demanded to know why?! Tell me why! Say something that explains away the pain, hurt, confusion and betrayal. As if the "why" would somehow change the "what".

In case you are thinking, "I know who she's talking about," let me explain that this cycle is about every time it happened. The cycle was always the same. So, I am not talking about none of my raggedy-ass, cheating exes, I am talking about my response to their raggedy asses cheating.

Therapy has taught me "you cannot control everything that happens to you, but you can control how you respond to it."

This is equal parts true and bullshit. You may not be able to control how you fall apart but you can supervise your healing journey.

In the black, lesbian community, we are all the things. We are friends, sisters, lovers, and enemies. We are both destroyer and architect of this community. We heal because we must; it is not a choice. We dust ourselves off and love again, ourselves and each other. Some of our healing is so personal. It happens only when we are alone. In the quiet of our mind we go back to those parts of ourselves we abandoned and beg for forgiveness. We heal in response to ourselves. Some of our healing requires sisterhood. As we love women, we are hurt by women and that affects our non-romantic relationships. It affects our ability to see one another as sisters. I believe our journeys back to sisterhood happen loudly. In social gatherings, over tea in our homes, during "just checking on you" phone calls, in group chats that buzz non-stop. That noisy sister-healing is loud and vibrates off the walls. It raises our vibrations. We heal in rhythm with one another. Then there is that complicated healing of the romantic heart. This healing is both private and dependent. It is the healing that teaches you what you need from you and what you need from others. It is and it ain't therapy. It is and it ain't beautiful. It is and it ain't traditional. It must be defined by you. No one can define your healing. No one can lead you to it. You have to make space for it, see it in the distance then pursue it relentlessly. Chase it like the first stud with locs you met at pride. Heal for the entire black lesbian community.

For this is the community you will find yourself and your soulmate.

I believe in the theory of soulmates. In a very Disney princess "one prince for one girl, the shoe will only fit the one" type of way. So, I heal for her. The one soulmate I know I deserve. We lose so much of ourselves along the way. In life and in love. We may not be virgins when we meet our soulmates. Our hearts will likely have scar tissue. Biases will have been created. Coping skills to tolerate, avoid, and accept pain will be in place. There will be impurities that need purging, sacred spaces that need clearing. We cannot wait until we met her to start this process. Be constantly combating everything that takes you away from you and her. Get that space in your head, heart, and home as clear as possible. Make your life comfortable for her as you make your way to one another. Know that she is on her way like you know your name. Say it aloud, believe it, own it. Heal for her.

Most importantly *heal for you*. You are your forever soulmate who cannot leave even if she tried. Heal you so you are ready for tomorrow. All the tomorrows good and bad. Lean into the sunshine as plants do. I won't cloud this with self-help suggestions. You are the only person that knows what your journey should be. Do not give into the temptation of following the paths of those around you. There is no shortcut, only constant, intentional, steady footwork. As you must heal to receive your soulmate, you must heal to receive everything that is meant for you. Sunshine, the taste of good food, the feel of a good shower are all experiences that feel better with a heart in healing. Heal because the hurt will come as it always has. Hurt destroys a person with too many untreated cracks, but it only causes temporary discomfort to a person intentional about healing.

Healing is an individual experience. For me, healing is about remaining receptive to love. The ability to experience hurt, to feel it, know that it is a very real possibility and continuing to seek love anyway, that is my healing. I heal through the lessons I learn through heartbreak. I heal by being accountable for the toxicity I bring to every relationship. I heal when I acknowledge the red flags I dismissed in the beginning. Heartbreak is the foundation for healing. Nothing unbroken is in need of repair. Rain and sunshine are both necessary for growth. Before hurt, I knew hope. After I experience hurt, I check to see if I feel that hope in my heart encouraging me to love, still. When I do not feel it, I know that I am not ready to date. I know that I need time to self-reflect. I know that intentional healing must be priority. So that I can get back to self-love, seeking love, and loving.

Healing is not a destination, it is an action that you must decide upon again and again...just like love. I celebrate the hurt and discomfort as the pathway to a better me.

Hurt

So you hurt me
After you said you wouldn't
More than said
After you promised you wouldn't
And I didn't believe you
So you promised again
You pushed and you repeated
You sacrificed you cried
And eventually I believed

So you hurt me
Only after I believed you

Well of course it was after
Guess you can't actually hurt a woman
Until after she is fully convinced that you won't
Until after she is ready to bet rent money
Her favorite scarf
Her grandmother's recipes
Her heart
That you won't

Because when a woman first meets you
She already knows that you will hurt her
That she cannot take it again
So she is resistant
But you are patient

You wait to get to the after

Then you do what you came to do
What I knew you'd do
What you have always done
The you that is you
And the you that was before you
And before you again

You got past all that
And you hurt me after
Aftermath
After the fact
After this
What happens?

I cannot leave as you did
So you hurt me
Must become
So what now
So I'll go on
'Til after becomes a beginning
Again

I Am Only

I cannot outrun my damages
Ignore my flaws
Act like this blood ain't stain my sheets and skin
Won't pretend
That I am less than human
Because you treated me that way

Take a Lover

My bed is a still place
Where nothing moves
There is too much room
And cold air

The nothing isn't so bad
My bed once hosted lies and resentment
So the nothing doesn't break me
But I think I've lain with it enough

I know that I must take a lover
Even after I have held my children
Tight in my arms
After loving them
Staying up all night
Catering and responding to their needs
I am still full of catering and responding

I know that I must take a lover
After I've read as many poems as my bookshelf can hold
Watched every love story my tube can offer
I can hear the absence of
"Baby do you need anything"
Ring in my head

There are affirmations on the wall above my bed
And a mirror on the vanity
I see myself there
As much as I love the image
I know that I must take a lover

I want to remember what my reflection
Looks like in the eyes of a woman
Who only sees me during the bewitching hours

This world has not convinced me
That dying alone is some badge of honor
Some proof that I didn't need anybody
I am not interested in doing bad by myself

I am past the point of crying about it
But I am also past the point of living it
I am a woman
Who is without a lover
Who desires to be loved
Who must, without apology take a lover

Bed

When you are single
Sometimes climbing into bed
Will feel like a confirmation of your nothingness

Will remind you of yo' mama yelling
you came here alone you gon' leave here alone

It will sometimes
Feel like practice
For laying cold and still
Alone in a grave
But ain't it home

Let your single woman sheets teach you
How your lover should wait for you
Patient and unchanging
Sheets that reach for you only
A place that calls your name

Offering warmth on nights that you smell like lemongrass
Or forgiveness those nights you're too tired to shower
Listen for your heartbeat
Let the rhythm raise the room's vibrations

That is how you call your lover
Rest your tongue
Rest your soul
Enjoy the empty
It is not forever

Fall

I yearn for the day I fall
And I don't mean in love
I mean the day I actually
Walk in our house, arms full of groceries
Distracted by the baby crying
Your Tims are in the middle of the floor again
After I've asked you to stop leaving your shoes everywhere
I don't see them
I trip and I fall

Our grocery bags spill over
They don't rip
'Cuz they're hemp…a few years ago we switched to cloth bags to respect mother nature
You see
We have been together long enough to have made a decision a few years ago

And I've asked you to keep these Tims out the middle floor
6 winters now
This means I've loved you at least 24 seasons
Means our summer-shine was always on its way
Our winters are fleeting and we've had April showers in our bedroom
Enough times to water every tulip on the road to Mecca

I've asked you to keep these Tims out the middle of the floor so no one would trip
And didn't it come true
Ain't I always right (except when I'm wrong)

Wasn't I right when I journaled about you after our first date
When I told my homegirls you were the one
When I starting looking into your eyes and never looked back…not once

I yearn for the day I fall
And the floor feels solid, and stable, like it could hold me forever
When the floor feels a lot like your love
I'm praying for the day I hit the floor and lay there a while
No rush to rise …no rush at all
Confusing our toddler with my laughter
Myself with my irritation and appreciation
For the fall that happens so many years after the fall in love

The fall that might hurt my hip
But never my heart
The fall that reminds me you
You are everything, except a nigga that puts shoes away
And if this is my biggest complaint
Praise Allah for I am blessed

Beautiful

I notice her not noticing other women
Never a lingering glance at a waitress
No double looks at passers by

Respect shouldn't feel this foreign
Compliments shouldn't feel this…suspicious

My self-esteem hasn't found its center yet
Some days she calls me beautiful
And I nod in agreement
I accept the compliment
Let it land on collarbone and assist with holding my head up

Some days she calls me beautiful
And I cower in uncomfortable disbelief
I shrink in the weight of the lie
I reject the accusation
And it hits me where I cannot bear

My self-esteem has not found its center yet
I don't know if I'm actually beautiful
But she's so honest
And seems so sure of it
I'm tempted to believe it
Or at least believe her

I don't know if I'm beautiful
But I shouldn't debate her
She says beautiful
I hear a lie

Maybe I am ugly
Ugly in the sense I turn her words into daggers
So they feel familiar

My self-esteem has not found its center yet
But in the meantime I've found her
I am trying to push away my demons
Before they push her away

I'm learning I cannot be loved
Until I believe I am lovable
I do not want to drain her
By demanding she keep pouring into a vase with a hole in it
A large gaping hole
Created so many moons before her compliments
Starting trying to fill me

My self esteem
Or lack thereof is exhausting
For me and for her

She hasn't decided that I am
Not worth the trouble yet
And I haven't convinced myself
To believe her words
Over my history

My self-esteem hasn't found its center yet
I want to lean into her
Let the weight of her words balance me

I want to be beautiful like her

Believe in love
In us
In my one day
Being able to hear beautiful
And know that it is true

SIX

hello, Big Homie . . .

SIX

hello, Big Homie . . .

THE REFORMED fuck boi...Hello, BIG HOMIE

I almost didn't write this section. I hate pushing highly unlikely false hope narratives. The hope of the reformed fuckboi is perhaps the most dangerous place for any femme to put her faith. Not because it does not happen. Fuckboi reform absolutely happens. Just do not get too excited, sis...you have absolutely nothing to do with it.

    I would imagine lying, cheating, and manipulating women starts to take a toll. I suspect the constant flow of femme tears starting a new rain shower of heartache before the last one dries up, causes a mildew smell after a while. I know studs are, in fact, human. Many are not psychopaths. At some point, the cries of the women they have hurt must echo in their sleep, haunt their dreams, and demand a lifestyle change. In a frantic effort to outrun their own karma they choose a woman and spoil her.

This woman usually fits into one of two categories. Category 1 Ride or Die Shorty. This woman has been around taking their shit for years. Sometimes in the capacity of an on again/off again lover. Sometimes in the position of a friend who has always been waiting and wishing, a-hoping and a-dreaming for her one chance at the spot! Or Category 2: Brand New Bitch. Brand new bitch is usually (but not always) younger or from out of town. Yes, this obviously allows the stud a clean state. But it also means that the brand new bitch is going to naturally be at a place of higher tolerance for bullshit. Being young and malleable or away from your support system creates a situation of dependency.

Young and/or isolated women are perfect transition women for fuckbois seeking an exit from their fuckboi life. They may or may not stay with these women. These women are a "fork in the road" experience. Meaning, after the stud in question has committed to this one woman, she begins practicing the habit of monogamy. She learns to be present in a relationship. She feels some relief from the juggling of women and the guilt of causing harm. Once the stud has had this experience, she has a choice to make. Go back to her old ways, possibly becoming a career fuckboi. Or use her knowledge of women and newfound decency to become...the rare, the necessary, the forever popping BIG HOMIE!!!!

When studs chooses the Big Homie path they often break up with the transition woman. This break-up begins their journey toward Big Homie behavior. For the first time, they handle the break-up responsibly. Once they get to a point where they are being honest with self and accountable for their actions, they desire the type of women who will also demand honesty, transparency and accountability. Being a fuckboi means finding a woman's weak spot and exploiting it. Being a Big Homie means learning a woman's weak spot and protecting it, even from themselves.

I want to be clear for my femme sisters. *You cannot create a Big Homie.* You cannot reform a fuckboi. They change for them not for you. Just as a stud subjecting you to toxic behavior is not your fault and does not say anything about your worth, neither does catching a stud in the Big Homie time in their life. They do not suddenly meet a "deserving woman" and catapult themselves into change. Big Homie-ness comes from within. I will say both fuckboi and Big Homie alike are strategic. Especially concerning the women they approach. Sis, if you are constantly being approached by fuckbois you have to acknowledge the energy you are using to attract your partner. We know that people often use sexual energy to attract partners. We lead with many different types of energy though. We may be using the lure of pity, or sympathy to pull someone in. For example, if we energetically pull lovers toward us with our desire to cater to someone we may draw a lover who is also catering; conversely we may draw in a lover who is dependent. What I'm saying is, we must be mindful of what part of ourselves we are using to attract our lovers. If you want a stud in their Big Homie phase, you are going to need to be putting out Big Homie meals.

That said, every Big Homie is a stud that has experienced a fuckboi stage, desired a change, then started practicing accountability and minimizing the hurt they leave in the world.

All Big Homies have a fuckboi past. They will share with you the parts that they deem relevant. They won't tell you everything about that phase. (Trust me, sis, do not dig; it is better to know less.) Like I said before, studs ain't shit, every single last one of 'em. Do not think you done lucked up and found a good nigga who did not have to go through the fuckboi stage to be a good nigga. Let me end this myth right now. What you have in your hands is a nigga that was never popping enough to be a fuckboi outwardly. Usually not attractive, beige personality having, money keep the lights on but no extras, weak-ass nigga. The issue here is, the second this weak-ass nigga has an opportunity to show out, she absolutely will. She may find her fuckboi confidence from a new job, the ability to bag you or a late-in-life glow up. But if it has not happened yet, it will. You cannot shortcut to Big Homie.

So, how do I know if this nigga a Big Homie?
Being the Big Homie cannot start and end with romantic partners. Do not ask if she is a Big Homie. Ask the women and children.

Does she have broke best friends (kids)? Every grown-ass masculine woman should be active in the lives of a child(ren). While most studs do not have kids (s/o stud mamas), do her nieces and nephews call? Does her god-baby blow her up while y'all out? Has she ever had to cancel a weekend because she promised the kids a pool party? The presence of kids in her life teach her to be accountable to people who can only offer love in return. Can she love selflessly and without expectation? Will she go out of her way to create whimsical moments of happiness just to see a smile? Ask the babies! Now, be mindful that studs are often present in the lives of ex-girlfriend's kids. This is usually a sign of a dependency issue and a messy situation. If there is any type of adult emotional dependency or void of respect between the adults in an "I'm helping my ex with her kid(s)", this is actually a lil' nigga situation. This DOES NOT count.

Does she visit her mama? I use "mama" loosely. Meaning, does she visit whatever woman loved, raised, and nurtured her? This can be a tricky one. Bums tend to visit their mamas and grandmas a lot, so be mindful of the who/what/why of the visits. Does she go to take granny to church? Is she making sure her mom remembered to lock her windows? Do they love to see her coming? Did auntie have a "special plate" for her "special baby." If she is a Big Homie, you will see the pride all in mom's face when she goes to visit. If she's a bum mama 'n'em gone be looking drained in the face, and in time, sis, *so will you*.

Now, if you have indeed been blessed to find a Big Homie, enjoy. Let go of any resentment from any of your old relationships. Let go of any jealousy about her old bitches. Enjoy your win; focus in on her and y'all and enjoy. This could be the beginning of forever.

I would say you get me everything I ask for
Except I never have to ask for it
So you give me the joy
Of never having to ask

Full

You fill the room
My head
My belly
These walls
In your absence you take up
Space

You're an urban girl's fantasy
A group chat legend
A happily ever after that begins again
Each morning
All night
Every text message

My sheets hold on to your scent
Until you come again
Make me cum, again

Filling the valley
Between my thighs
With your hands
Fingers curving upward
Sending me into a spiral

My tongue makes space
For only one name
Your name
So beautiful
It fills my…
It fills me

The Women

If you did not love me
As you do
I might be bothered by the women

The women who stare at you with lust
Sometimes bold enough to tell me
How wonderful you are
In a tone that suggest
I am undeserving

You love me
In a way that helps other women
Realize what they desire
So I cannot blame the women
Who want you

You love me in a way
That turns my jealousy into empathy
Tells me that the women
Want you for your looks
Not just your "good looks"
But for the way you look at me
The looks they see you give me
As I walk beside you

They don't just want you
They want you to want them
Being the object of your desire
Means something

Speaking as the woman
Who is covered by you
I can tell you
Your love makes the ground stop shaking
You make the pavement rise to greet my feet

Even when you are not in the room
It is filled with the after light of your glow
It is warm wherever you are, wherever you leave

And this world is such a cold place
I do not blame the women who want your warmth
In fact I am one

SEVEN

her name means charming . . .

SEVEN

her name means charming . . .

Flowers 3 - Her and Me

Her (Sahir Al-Salam, Via: Facebook, August 28, 2019)

> I buy her flowers often to keep her smiling when I'm not around
> I'm not perfect but my flowers never come with an apology
>
> More like:
> *Thanks for the other night, babe*
> *Thanks for being a good woman*
> *Thanks for being an even better friend*
> *Thanks for silently investing in me when I would never ask*
> *Thanks for loving me the way you do*
>
> *Congratulations on your book*
> *Congrats on your promotion*
> *Congrats on your raise*
>
> Again, flowers are a regular thing because she is always being great

Me (Nkenge)

You don't offer roses as an apology
Never make them hold their petals
Down in shame

Your roses come to me
Standing their true height
Announcing themselves
With flower and thorn
Beautiful and honest

This is what rose oil smells like
When it isn't interrupted
By the stench of broken promises
Fragrant and free

You give me roses
That are only roses
That don't double as
Announcements of failure
You give me roses that
Never make me regret
You, our love, these flowers
You give me
Roses

Queen Charming

While I was living out of state, I was dealing with the toughest bout of depression I had ever experienced in my life. In an effort to save my sanity, I threw myself into writing and my design company. I started to pay more attention to other small business owners. Also, I began to seek friendships with other black women entrepreneurs on my Friends List. There was one woman in particular I kept asking myself, how is it that we don't know each other? We knew the same people, had socialized in the same places, grew up in the same Detroit, and somehow never met. Anyway, we first discussed our businesses. She was so easy to talk to and filled with positivity that our friendship quickly became a source of light in my life. Our friendship was also very comfortable for me because I had sworn off fuckboi studs. Now Friend was fine, but not on my radar. Friend had fuckboi locs, fuckboi tattoos, fuckboi cadence when she spoke, drove a truck, wore gray joggers and fuckboi mesh running shoes. No, thank you. Anyway, she was cool as hell. I enjoyed talking to her. She provided a space for me to speak freely, without judgment. She did not interject her opinions on my decisions; I never felt judged.

She listened and she celebrated all of my small victories, like eating or getting out the house or staying calm. Every morning she would text me my horoscope. I am not well-versed in astrology, but her sending my horoscope at that time in my life allowed me to feel the sun and admire the moon. Depression was telling me I was worthless, and no one would notice if I were not alive anymore. (Depression is a cold bitch.) My horoscope reminded me that I was given the gift of life. As I did not decide which sunrise I was born under, I could not decide my own sunset. I would look for signs of my horoscope to be true throughout the day. This allowed my brain to focus on something other than the madness I was living. Her taking time to text me every morning conveyed to me that I was connected to other people and that my existence mattered.

I started to read the horoscope aloud in the mirror every morning. Eventually, I was well enough to start saying affirmations. Alhamduillah, she was sent to me at the most necessary time. I hope she knows what her kindness did for me. She was a lighthouse, guiding me back to myself and my home.

When Summer '18 came, I relocated back home to Detroit a single woman. My friend, Queen Charming, and I hung out daily. She genuinely thought I was a dope person and wanted me to find my happiness. This is important: I said she wanted me to find my happiness, not she wanted to make me happy. During the friendship stage of our journey together, everyone around us made assumptions about our intentions with each other. And for months they were wrong, well wrong at the time. The week before the "full-table talk" I caught myself not stopping myself. I had been able to acknowledge everything amazing about her without desiring it, until I did. We started to hug as we departed from each other, one day she held on a bit longer than a friend would. And I just fell into it. I did not stop myself from smelling her cologne, the warmth of her locs, how her arms wrapped around me. One hand reaching upward spine while the other rested lower back keeping me in place.

When I went into my father's house that night not knowing what to do with myself, I sat in the chair by the window and watched her drive off. I got online and there was a meme of a beautiful lesbian couple in the shower kissing. One brown skin and feminine, the other light complexion with locs and tattoos. I thought there was a resemblance and, laughing out loud, I reposted the meme. Queen Charming screenshot the picture back to me with the message, "Who this look like?" She also noticed the resemblance. We had about four more text exchanges and she abruptly stopped the conversation by texting, "we need to talk, lunch tomorrow." Tomorrow came, she picked me up. We went to this little city with a strip of restaurants; tried to find the best one. We were both indecisive as hell ultimately just stopping at the last restaurant on the strip, out of options.

We sat and ordered our food, then the waitress just kept coming back with food that we didn't order compliments of the chef. Turns out Queen Charming knew the chef. This is what being out with her was like. Things just fell into place always in her favor. She started the conversation, told me that she had more than friend feelings for me. I returned the sentiment. She went on to tell me there was no pressure and she would accept a friendship if that is all I wanted. I told her again of my more than friend feelings. At a random restaurant we stumbled upon happenstance, behind a table full of every food the chef had to offer we agreed to begin dating.

The way she handled the whole thing raised my dating expectations and laid the foundation for our intimate communication. That night before when we were texting, she intentionally cut the conversation short. We both knew we needed to talk. Had we continued texting the conversation may have happened via text. That would have cheapened the experience. You cannot edit an experience, but she always gets it right the first time. In true Big Homie form she made time for us, sat me down, made eye contact, made her intentions clear and did not mince words. She didn't hold a secret a crush, hiding behind the guise of friendship. When our friendship shifted, she acknowledged that, bold, fearless and with precision. She never misses an opportunity to do things right and to make moments memorable.

And so our dating journey began. I told the group chat first.

Me: *so we're dating now*

Friend 1: *y'all been dating but awwwww*

Friend 2: *she's so lit ol' aye we need to talk looking ass*

Me: *girl I didn't know what the fuck she was about to say. I was shook af trying to read that menu*

Friend 2: *what if you found the one non-fuckboi unicorn*

Friend 1: *on some happily ever after shit*

Me: *that's funny, did I tell y'all her name literally means charming…*

Flowers

Remember that day we met for breakfast in Ferndale.

We walked along the strip of restaurants trying to guess which place had the most vegetarian options. It was summer. There were flower beds outside of each restaurant. I noticed you reach out for one and as silly as this sounds, I held my breath and feared for that flower's life. You grabbed it, enveloped its entirety in your hand. I watched the flower recoil and disappear in your hand. Then, all at once, you opened your hand. The flower sprung back to life unharmed. In this moment I knew I needed to fuck you.

I saw your need to touch the flower for all its softness and beauty. More importantly, I saw that you didn't allow your desire to become the flowers demise. And something about the way the petals sprung back into place after such a firm grasp told me you knew when to/how to wrap your hand around my neck with steady dominance and when to release for air.

Please, always treat me like that flower.

Flowers II

I buy flowers almost every week
I set them centerpiece on the dining room table
The nights you don't stay over I set them on my nightstand
Flowers are one of those creations Allah made for no other reason
Than to display artistry and beauty

You've spoiled me in this way

I wake up next to them and remember to praise Allah
I wake up next to you I see art and beauty
So on nights I know you won't be there in the morning
I place the flowers there
Because if I can't have you
Only flowers will do

Sunshine

You are out of town again
Atlanta this time
In a moment of missing you
I opened my curtain to let the sun in
Lay across my bed

The rays found me
Traveled up my legs
Slowly decided on a resting place
And stayed there

Warmed my thighs enough to let me know
I'd be cold when I left this bed but
Not so warm that it caused discomfort
I lay there and closed my eyes

This only caused me to miss you more
When you are home and we are in your bed
Your hand finds my thigh
Finds its resting spot
Makes me warm, just warm enough

Did you send those rays my way?
Tell them just how to touch me
I'm not sure if you are like the sun
Or if the sun like you?

But you both always come back
Just when I need you

Before the missing turns to misery
Come...back...soon
There is only so much the sun can do in your absence

Chai tea

We kissed
I sucked your bottom lip
It tasted like cinnamon

Maybe because I'd just had chai tea
Or maybe your bottom lip actually tastes like cinnamon

I don't know which is true
But either way
Cinnamon will always remind me of your kisses

I drink chai tea way too much for this
I hope your lips are always these reminders of my favorite tea
Always a place where honey lives
Always a thing I can't get enough of

Always available to me
In the morning
And nights I can't sleep
Smelling of cinnamon
With a promise of relaxation

Crop

My body welcomes you the way a crop suffering a heat wave
Beckons a thunderstorm
Like….my God I need this
Like …where have you been
Like…never make me wait this long again

You storm gentle enough to please petals
But hard enough to saturate roots

Stopping just before I completely forget about the heat wave
Leaving me in a state of satisfaction and gratitude

Night in NOLA

I realized it suddenly at dinner
We were in that Italian place with the cute balcony
But carpet so dingy
We knew the food would be average at best
You couldn't decide what to order

Rarely are you…unsure
But that menu
Simple as it was
Seemed to wear on you

I, on the other hand
Ordered without hesitation
Leaving me time to exam the night

We found this place walking aimlessly through Frenchmen St.
I walked a tiny historic sidewalk
In heels
Surrounded by drunks and hungry dogs
Had not a care in the world
I realized
You had been shape shifting with every step

When we passed the angry drunken men
You made yourself palmetto tree
Allowing me to only see the beauty of the city

When we passed the hungry dogs
You made yourself
An impassable fence they dare not approach

The entire walk
You were ten steps ahead
Already protecting me
From the dangers that might be
But also right next to me
Your hand in mine

My only concern
Rain puddles and pasta
By the time we sat down to eat
You must have been exhausted

I didn't have the words that night
But I need you to know
I am most grateful
For what you give
And the walks you've allowed uninterrupted

Your protection doesn't announce itself
Doesn't yell pounding its chest
Demanding attention

Your protection
Is executed with such grace
I forget that danger exist at all
Oblivious blissful sing-song
Dance-in-the-rain
Freedom

You give me moments that women dream of
That our ancestors died for
Moments that rest between

Enchantment and euphoria

So sometimes
Menus will just fucking exhaust you
Take your time
As you have with me
As I will with you
I'll take my time with you
Forever
If you give it to me

Love-Her

I have found a lover
She taste like a flower that never had to ask for rain twice
That bees avoided because honey ought not be that sweet
Whose petals never compromised themselves to get to the sun
Her roots are wild and uninhibited
She's learned to survive in rolling fields and under concrete
I love her the same way flowers turn yellow
Intentional, with bliss
The same way the wave rushes toward the shore
And then a little more

She tastes me like she is burying a seed
And will be back to harvest the fruit
Fucks me like
The crops need saturating and
I am the only rain cloud in the sky

Like there is no other option
Like it was always Allah's plan
Like here sunshine here I am

I have found a lover worth writing home about
My home has always been in books
So I'll write of her here
This way she is always home
Always with me

Here

I knew you were here
Even when I wasn't sure if you actually existed
I knew if you did
You'd be from here
You'd have roots here
You'd understand mine (and me)

In this city
Where I gained my footing
Walked barefoot in backyards
Walked sidewalks in heels
Ran away from and toward

I knew you'd be here
If a woman like you existed
She'd be so fucking Detroit
She'd be four seasons in one day
She'd be thick as traffic on 94 during rush hour
She would know that flowers sometimes grow in the
Front yards of abandoned houses
She'd see beauty differently

When I left here
Lived in that city I almost died in
I didn't think I'd make it back home

I met you when I was there
And you were here

I have always been a girl
Who daydreamed too often
Admired the princesses
And believed
In love, in soulmates, in Prince Charming

We both grew up here
Same streets same clubs
Same winters same waters
Within feet of each other
I'm sure I've felt you
But the first time I heard you
We had 638 miles between us

And I wished I were there
You told me if I ever found my way back
You'd show me how nothing changes the sun here
Told me you'd be pulling up
White horse style
Except we in the city, so white truck

And you did
Baby, you did everything you ever said you would
Remember that night you told me
You liked driving east because you can only smell the water on the Eastside
I lived here forever and never noticed it
It was so clear and fragrant
How had I not noticed that in 3 decades, here

Maybe I didn't need it 'til that summer
You can only notice something

For the first time
One time
The smell of the river
The dimple in your chin
The curve of your index finger (especially the left hand)

Here we are
Here we grew
Here is home
And I am finally here, with you

thank ya's

My editor Alana Gracey for all the patience, grace and skill you offer. (We did it again!!)

Alexis Sims of Whatever Media for formatting and reminding me that this is a business.

BL Bronson for the interview that helped me complete the BDE essay. I appreciate your conversation and friendship...you da homie.

Patty-Cake and Tink for teaching me that you can be a selfish asshole sometimes and still deserve love.

To all of my online friends who laugh and love with me, thanks for the encouragement

And of course #Bunbae for...e v e r y t h i n g.

Made in the USA
Columbia, SC
16 March 2021